# RYLAN VEXOR

# Habits of a Kind Leader

*The Daily Habits That Transform Teams and Drive Success*

# Contents

# 1

# Introduction

Leadership. It's a word we throw around a lot, but how often do we truly stop to ask: *What does it actually mean to be a leader?* And, more importantly, how do you build a leadership style that not only inspires your team, but makes them *better*, more productive, and efficient?

Here's the truth! Being a great leader isn't about putting on some tough guy persona or pretending to be someone you're not. It's about owning who you are, stepping into your power, and understanding that leadership can be both *assertive* and *kind*. That's right. **Kindness. It's not a weakness. It's a superpower**.

This book is about how to build a team that thrives because the people who work with you are not robots or pawns in some game. They're human beings with ambitions, strengths, and struggles. And the best way to bring out the best in them is by combining assertiveness and kindness, two traits that are often seen as opposites but are, in my point of view, the perfect leadership combo. This isn't just about getting people to do what you want. This is about inspiring people to do their best work, because they trust you, because they respect you, and because you're helping them be the best version of themselves.

Let me tell you something: ***You don't need to change who you are to be a great leader.*** I know the pressure and the constant feeling that you have to play the game and conform to what your boss or the industry thinks a leader should be. I've been there. And I've seen it in countless others. The idea that to be assertive, to be respected, you've got to be tough, intimidating, and, yes, sometimes rude. I call BS on that.

You don't have to shout, belittle, or talk down to people to make them respect you or listen to you. If anything, that approach leads to fear, mistrust, and disengagement. The best teams, high-performing teams, are built on trust. They're not built on fear. They're not built on playing power games. They're built on strong relationships where people feel seen, heard, and understood.

That's where kindness comes in. But here's the kicker: Kindness doesn't mean being a pushover. It doesn't mean being soft or timid. Kindness means giving people the space to express themselves, to fail and learn, and to feel like their contribution matters. And being assertive means clearly communicating your expectations and holding people accountable to high standards without resorting to manipulation or fear-based tactics.

You have to lead from your heart and your head. And most

importantly, ***you have to lead as yourself***. Not as someone else's version of a leader. The moment you start adapting your style to fit someone else's idea of what a leader should look like, you're doing yourself, your team, and your mission a disservice. That's when the magic happens: When you stop pretending to be someone you're not and lean into the strength of who you really are.

The truth is, your unique way of leading, your natural combination of assertiveness and kindness, is exactly what will make your team not just efficient but unstoppable. This book will give you the tools to build that kind of leadership and to bring out the best in everyone around you.

So let's get into it. **Get ready to lead the way you've always known you could: assertive, kind, and unapologetically you.**

## My Experience as a Kind Leader

I started out as a Stock Management Technician at a retail company. Looking back, I can say that my journey was shaped not by titles or formal promotions, but by the way my team and I worked together. To be honest, I didn't go seeking leadership, it almost felt like I was chosen by the people around me.

I wasn't the loudest voice in the room but I was always there, competent, dynamic, and resilient. I had this energy that never let me back down from a challenge. I faced every obstacle with a smile, and no matter how tough things got, my team could always count on me to bring a positive attitude and deliver results. Even when things weren't going perfectly, I rarely let them see me falter. I wanted to be a source of strength for the group and as I took on more responsibility things began to evolve quickly.

I realized that leadership is not always comfortable. It tests you. It pushes your limits. You're constantly faced with situations that make you question yourself and your choices. There was a point in the company's journey when we went through a major process overhaul, and I had to communicate to my team that what we were doing wasn't working anymore. We had to change, adapt, and do things differently if we wanted to see better results. It was a challenging phase, and honestly, it was the time when I questioned myself the most. I remember those moments of self-doubt vividly. I'd ask myself, "Is this really my path?" "Am I doing the right thing by pushing my team to change?" "Wouldn't it be easier to just go back to being a technician, where I felt more comfortable?" The pressure was intense and my boss even once told me I was "too nice and kind with people". I often wondered if I was truly cut out for leadership. There were days when I tried to mold myself into something I wasn't and tried to fit the image of what others thought a leader should be.

But those moments of doubt were also the moments when I learned the most about myself. I realized there's no one-size-fits-all leadership style. People and organizations require different approaches. Leadership isn't about having all the answers. It's about guiding your team through challenges, empowering them, and celebrating their victories.

2

# The Foundation of Kindness and Assertiveness

At the heart of great leadership is a powerful balance: kindness and assertiveness. These two traits, when used together, create a leadership style that's real, effective, and respected. In this section, we'll dig into why these traits are so important, why being yourself is non-negotiable as a leader, and how trying to fit into someone else's idea of leadership can backfire. We'll also talk about why being rigid in your approach can hurt your team more than help it.

## Understanding the Power of Kindness in Leadership

Think about it this way! When you lead with kindness, you're creating an environment where people feel safe, valued, and motivated. And when people feel good about where they work, they show up and deliver at a higher level.

**Picture this:** You've got someone on your team who's missing deadlines or just not performing the way they used to. The old-school "tough" leader might call them out in a meeting or send a harsh email demanding better results. But what if, instead, you pull them aside and say, "Hey, I've noticed you've been struggling lately. Is everything okay? How can I help?" That simple shift in approach can uncover the real problem: maybe they're dealing with personal stuff, or maybe they're confused about what's expected of them. **Showing you care doesn't mean you're letting them off the hook. It means you're leading with humanity first.**

Kindness also has this ripple effect. When you celebrate people's wins, no matter how small, it sends a message: *I see you, and I appreciate you.* Whether it's a shoutout during a meeting, a handwritten note, or even just a quick **"You crushed it on that project"** those moments of recognition can make a huge impact. It's not about handing out fake compliments, it's about being real and specific. **That kind of kindness doesn't just make people feel good, it fuels them to do better.**

## The Role of Assertiveness in Leadership

**If kindness is the heart of leadership, assertiveness is the backbone.** Being assertive is about saying what needs to be said, clearly and confidently, without stepping on anyone else in the process. It's the difference between a leader who waffles on decisions and one who inspires trust because they know where they're going and why.

Let's say your team is stuck in a debate about which direction to take on a big project. As the leader, it's your job to listen to everyone's input but at some point, you have to step in and say,

"Here's what we're doing, and here's why." That's assertiveness. You're not shutting people down, you're giving them clarity. And clarity is what builds trust.

Be careful because being assertive doesn't mean being a jerk. It's not about barking orders or always having the last word. It's about setting expectations and holding people accountable in a way that's fair and respectful. Like, instead of saying, "I need this done now," try saying, "This is a priority. Can you commit to having it done by Friday?" See the difference? You're still being direct, but you're also being considerate.

Assertiveness also means being willing to say no. This one's hard for a lot of leaders, especially when you're trying to please everyone. But here's the truth: if you say yes to everything, you're going to stretch your team too thin and burn them out. Saying no isn't about being difficult, it's about protecting your team's focus and energy so they can crush the things that really matter.

## Why Leadership Doesn't Mean Playing a Role

One of the biggest mistakes leaders make is trying to be something they're not. Maybe you've had a boss who was super strict and no-nonsense, and you think, "That's what leadership looks like." So, you try to copy their style even though it feels totally wrong for you. The result? Your team sees right through it, and you end up feeling exhausted and disconnected.

Authenticity is everything in leadership. People don't want a leader who's playing a role, they want someone who's real. If you're naturally empathetic and collaborative, lean into that. If you're more analytical and structured, own it. **Whatever your style, it works best when it's true to who you are.**

Being authentic doesn't mean you stop growing or improving. It means you're not pretending to be someone you're not. If you're unsure about how to lead in a certain situation, admit it! Saying, "I don't have all the answers, but let's figure this out together," shows strength, not weakness. It shows your team that you're human and that makes them more likely to trust and follow you.

## The Consequences of a Rigid Leadership Style

Here's the harsh reality: if you're rigid in your leadership, you're going to lose people. Teams thrive on flexibility, creativity, and the freedom to experiment. A leader who insists on doing things one way, their way, shuts down all of that.

Take micromanaging, for example. Maybe you think keeping a close eye on every detail will ensure quality, but what it really does is kill your team's confidence and make them feel like you don't trust them. Over time, that kind of leadership leads to disengagement and, eventually, turnover. Nobody wants to work for a leader who doesn't give them room to grow.

Rigid leadership also clings to outdated ideas, like the myth that being "tough" equals being respected. **Sure, fear might get short-term results, but it doesn't build loyalty or long-term success**. A better approach? Be firm when you need to be, but always pair it with support. For example, if someone's falling behind, address the issue directly, but also offer a solution: "This isn't where we need to be. Let's talk about how we can get back on track." That balance of accountability and encouragement is what separates good leaders from great ones.

The bottom line? Rigid leadership might feel safe, but it's holding you back. When you let go of the need to control everything and start trusting your team, amazing things happen. People step up. Ideas flow. Results follow.

Leadership built on kindness and assertiveness isn't just a nice idea, it's a game-changer. When you lead with empathy and clarity, authenticity and adaptability, you set the stage for a team that's not only high-performing but also deeply connected to the mission. This is the foundation that every great leader needs to build on, and it starts with showing up as your best self, every single day.

3

# Building the Foundation for Kind Leadership

L eadership isn't just about what you say or the decisions you make, it's about the culture you create and the example you set. To build the kind of leadership that truly connects with people, you need a strong foundation. That foundation is built on trust, clarity, emotional intelligence, and leading in a way that aligns with your values every single day. Let's dive into what it takes to create this foundation and why it's the key to becoming the kind of leader people want to follow.

## Creating a Culture of Trust Through Transparency

**If leadership is the engine that drives a team, trust is the fuel that keeps it running.** Without trust, even the most talented teams can stall, lose momentum, or fail altogether. Transparency is how you build that trust. It's about being open, honest, and real with your team sharing the good, the bad, and the uncomfortable in a way that keeps everyone informed and engaged.

The beauty of transparency is that it removes the guesswork. When people know where they stand and what's happening around them, they can focus on their work instead of worrying about hidden agendas or potential surprises. It's not just a feel-good practice, it's a strategic leadership move that fosters loyalty, improves communication, and creates a strong foundation for collaboration.

**Why Transparency Matters**

Imagine you're part of a team facing uncertain times: maybe budget cuts, restructuring, or even layoffs. Leaders often shy away from addressing tough topics because they don't want to create panic. **But silence creates its own problems.** When there's a lack of information, people fill in the blanks with worst-case scenarios. Rumors start, morale drops, and productivity tanks.

Now imagine a leader who tackles the situation head-on: "Here's what's happening. It's not ideal, but we're working on solutions, and here's what you can expect next." That kind of candor doesn't magically solve the problem, but it builds trust because the leader chooses honesty over avoidance. When people feel included in the conversation, they're more likely to stick with you through the tough times.

Transparency isn't just about navigating challenges, it's also about celebrating successes and giving credit where it's due. When you openly recognize the efforts and contributions of your team, you reinforce trust and strengthen relationships. For instance, instead of taking credit for a project's success, a transparent leader might say, "This wouldn't have been possible without the team's creativity and hard work." That small acknowledgment goes a long way in building a culture of respect and appreciation.

## How to Practice Transparency in Leadership

Being transparent doesn't mean oversharing or dumping every detail on your team. It's about sharing the right information at the right time. Here are some practical ways to lead with transparency:

1. **Open Communication:** Keep your team in the loop with regular updates, whether it's through meetings, emails, or one-on-ones. Use these opportunities to explain the "why" behind decisions, not just the "what." For example, if you're shifting priorities, explain the reasoning so your team understands the bigger picture.

2. **Admit Mistakes:** Nobody's perfect, and pretending to be will only alienate your team. If you make a mistake, own it. Say something like, "I made the wrong call on this, and here's what I'm doing to fix it." Admitting mistakes shows humility and encourages your team to be honest about their own challenges.

3. **Create Space for Feedback:** Transparency is a two-way street. Invite your team to share their thoughts, concerns, and ideas. For instance, during a project review, you could ask, "What worked well, and what could we improve next time?" When people see that you value their input, they're more likely to trust you.

4. **Be Clear About Boundaries:** While transparency is vital, not everything can or should be shared. There will be times when you need to withhold certain details, whether

it's for confidentiality or to avoid unnecessary stress. The key is to be upfront about those boundaries. Instead of dodging a question, say, "I can't go into detail about that right now, but I'll share more as soon as I can."

## The Ripple Effect of Transparency

Transparency isn't just about you as a leader, it's about what it creates within your team. When you lead with openness, you set the tone for how others communicate and interact. Your honesty becomes a model for your team to follow.

For example, if you're transparent about a mistake you've made, it signals to your team that it's safe for them to do the same. Instead of hiding errors or blaming others, they'll feel comfortable owning up and working together to find solutions. This creates a culture of accountability and learning, where mistakes aren't punished but used as opportunities to grow.

Transparency also fosters stronger relationships. People are more likely to trust leaders who are genuine and straightforward. That trust builds loyalty, which translates into higher engagement and better performance. When team members trust their leader, they're more likely to speak up, take risks, and collaborate effectively because they know they're in a safe and supportive environment.

## Transparency as a Leadership Legacy

Ultimately, transparency is about legacy. When you build a culture of trust through openness and honesty, you're creating something that lasts. Teams move on, projects end, but the trust you build stays with the people you lead.

The leaders who stand out are the ones people remember and talk about years later. They are the ones who led with integrity and authenticity. They didn't hide behind corporate jargon or make decisions in secrecy. They showed up, told the truth, and treated their teams like partners, not subordinates.

Transparency isn't always easy. It takes courage to have difficult conversations and vulnerability to admit when you don't have all the answers. But the payoff is worth it. When you create a culture of trust through transparency, you're not just leading, you're building something bigger than yourself. And that's what real leadership is all about.

## Setting Clear Expectations and Holding People Accountable

Leadership thrives on clarity. When your team knows what's expected of them and how their work connects to the bigger picture, they're empowered to perform at their best. At the same time, accountability ensures that expectations don't just hang in the air. They turn into real, tangible results. These two concepts, clarity and accountability, work hand in hand to create a high-performing team culture. Let's break it down and explore how to put them into action.

**Why Clear Expectations Matter**

Imagine being asked to complete a task without any clear instructions. You're left guessing what's required, how success will be measured, or when it's due. Frustrating, right? Ambiguity like this can create unnecessary stress and waste valuable time. As a leader, your job is to eliminate that guessing game.

Clear expectations set the stage for success by giving people a roadmap. They outline what needs to be done, why it matters, and how it should be achieved. For example, instead of saying, "I need this report ASAP," a clear expectation would sound like, "I need a one-page summary of last quarter's sales data, focusing on trends and key insights. Can you have it ready by Thursday at 3 PM?"

Notice the difference? The second example removes uncertainty. It specifies the task, provides a deadline, and explains the purpose. This level of clarity not only reduces confusion but also increases the likelihood of high-quality results.

Clarity isn't just about tasks, it's also about roles and goals. Your team should understand their individual responsibilities and how their work fits into the team's overall objectives. When everyone knows their lane, collaboration becomes smoother, and you minimize overlaps or gaps in effort.

## The Power of Accountability

Once expectations are clear, accountability is what ensures they're met. But let's be real, accountability can get a bad rap. Too often, it's associated with finger-pointing, blame, or micromanaging. True accountability, however, is none of those things. It's about creating a culture where everyone takes ownership of their commitments and feels responsible for their part in the team's success.

To foster accountability, start by leading by example. If you commit to something, follow through. Your actions set the tone for your team. If they see you skipping deadlines or making excuses, they'll feel justified in doing the same. But when you consistently meet your commitments, you inspire them to do the same.

Accountability also involves open communication. If someone on your team is struggling to meet expectations, don't let it fester. Address the issue directly but constructively. For example, instead of saying, "You're always late with your work," try this: "I noticed the last two reports were submitted late, which impacted our ability to move forward on schedule. Is there something blocking you, and how can we address it together?"

**This approach turns accountability into a conversation, not a confrontation**. It focuses on finding solutions rather than assigning blame, which builds trust and helps your team grow.

**Practical Tips for Setting Expectations and Driving Accountability**

1. **Be Specific:** Generalities don't work when it comes to expectations. Instead of saying, "Do your best on this project," clarify what "best" looks like in measurable terms. For example, outline the scope, deliverables, deadlines, and quality standards.
2. **Document Expectations:** Whether it's through an email, a shared document, or project management software, put expectations in writing. This eliminates any confusion and serves as a reference point if questions arise later.
3. **Set Checkpoints:** Don't just set expectations and disappear until the deadline. Schedule regular check-ins

to monitor progress, provide feedback, and address any roadblocks. For example, during a team meeting, you might ask, "How are we progressing on the marketing campaign? Are there any challenges we need to address before the next milestone?"

4. **Acknowledge Successes:** When someone meets or exceeds expectations, celebrate it. A simple "Great job on delivering that project ahead of schedule made a big difference" reinforces positive behavior and motivates the team.

5. **Address Missed Expectations Promptly:** If a team member doesn't meet expectations, don't let it slide. The longer you wait, the harder the conversation becomes. Be direct but empathetic. For instance, "This presentation didn't align with the brief. Let's go over where it fell short and how we can improve it next time."

## The Bigger Picture

Setting clear expectations and holding people accountable does more than just improve individual performance, it elevates the entire team. When everyone knows what's expected and takes responsibility for their role, collaboration improves, goals are met more efficiently, and morale skyrockets.

But there's a deeper layer to this: clarity and accountability create trust. When people know you're clear about what you want and fair in how you hold them accountable, they feel respected and valued. They trust that you're not playing favorites, shifting the goalposts, or throwing them under the bus when things go wrong.

At its core, leadership is about guiding people toward a shared vision. Clear expectations are the map, and accountability is the compass that keeps everyone on course. When you master these two principles, you create a team culture that's not just productive but also resilient, motivated, and engaged. That's the kind of team that doesn't just hit goals, they surpass them.

## Self-Awareness and Emotional Intelligence

At the heart of effective leadership lies the ability to understand yourself and others. Self-awareness and emotional intelligence (EI) are not buzzwords, they're the foundation of connecting with your team, managing challenges, and making better decisions. Without them, leadership can become robotic, reactive, or disconnected. With them, you unlock the potential to inspire, empathize, and lead with authenticity.

### The Role of Self-Awareness in Leadership

Self-awareness starts with looking inward. It's about knowing your strengths, weaknesses, values, and triggers. Many leaders operate on autopilot, reacting instinctively to situations without understanding why they respond the way they do. But great leaders take the time to pause, reflect, and assess their own behavior.

Consider how you react under pressure. Maybe when a deadline looms, you become short-tempered, snapping at team members who are just trying to help. Or perhaps you avoid difficult conversations, hoping problems will resolve themselves. These are natural human tendencies, but they can undermine your leadership.

Self-awareness helps you recognize these patterns. When you understand how stress or feedback affects you, you can actively work to manage your reactions. For example, if you know you tend to shut down in conflict, you can prepare yourself to stay engaged by practicing active listening or taking a moment to breathe before responding.

A self-aware leader is also in tune with their blind spots. Nobody is good at everything, and pretending otherwise is a fast track to burnout or losing credibility. Being upfront about your limitations shows humility and opens the door for collaboration. For example, if you're not great with numbers, admitting it and leaning on a team member who excels in that area doesn't make you weak, **it makes you wise.**

## Emotional Intelligence: The Secret to Connection

If self-awareness is about understanding yourself, emotional intelligence is about understanding and connecting with others. It's the ability to recognize, interpret, and respond to the emotions of the people you work with. EI isn't just about being nice, it's about being tuned in to what's going on beneath the surface and responding in a way that builds trust and collaboration.

For instance, imagine one of your team members has been unusually quiet during meetings. A leader without emotional intelligence might brush it off or assume they're just disengaged. But a leader with EI would notice the change in behavior and take the time to check in: "Hey, I've noticed you've been quieter than usual lately. Is everything okay?" That small act of noticing and asking can make someone feel seen and supported, which strengthens your relationship.

Emotional intelligence also helps you navigate conflict. Instead of reacting defensively to criticism, you can pause, assess the other person's emotions, and respond thoughtfully. For example, if a team member expresses frustration about a decision you made, instead of saying, "That's just how it is," you might respond with, "I hear your concerns. Let's talk about why I made that decision and see if there's a way to address your worries." This approach diffuses tension and keeps the conversation productive.

**Building Self-Awareness and Emotional Intelligence**
Both self-awareness and emotional intelligence are skills you can develop with practice. Start by paying attention to your emotions and the emotions of others. Reflect on your reactions at the end of each day: what went well, what didn't, and why? Over time, you'll start noticing patterns and opportunities for growth.

Feedback is another powerful tool for self-awareness. Ask your team or peers for honest input about your leadership style. It might feel uncomfortable, but it's invaluable for understanding how others perceive you. For example, you might learn that your team appreciates your vision but feels you could communicate expectations more clearly. That insight gives you a roadmap for improvement.

To strengthen emotional intelligence, practice active listening. When someone speaks, focus entirely on what they're saying, without thinking about your response or getting distracted. Pay attention to their tone, body language, and word choice. This level of attention not only helps you understand their emotions but also shows them you value their perspective.

Empathy is another cornerstone of emotional intelligence. Put yourself in your team's shoes: how might they be feeling in a given situation? For example, if you've just announced a big change, consider the uncertainty or anxiety they might be experiencing. Address those feelings proactively: "I know this change might feel overwhelming, and I want to assure you that we're here to support you through it."

**The Impact of Self-Awareness and Emotional Intelligence**
When you lead with self-awareness and emotional intelligence, the ripple effects are profound. You create a culture where people feel understood, valued, and empowered to bring their full selves to work.

Teams led by emotionally intelligent leaders are often more cohesive and resilient. Instead of avoiding tough conversations, they tackle challenges head-on with a sense of trust and mutual respect. Instead of bottling up frustrations, they feel comfortable speaking openly, knowing they'll be heard.

For you as a leader, these skills are game-changers. They help you make better decisions, build stronger relationships, and navigate the complexities of leadership with confidence and grace. Self-awareness and emotional intelligence aren't just "nice-to-haves", they're essential tools for anyone who wants to lead with impact and heart.

In the end, leadership isn't about having all the answers or being the smartest person in the room. **It's about understanding yourself and others well enough to create an environment where everyone can succeed.** When you lead with self-awareness and emotional intelligence, you're not just managing a team, you're inspiring a movement.

## Leading by Example: The Power of Consistency

Leadership isn't just about the words you say, it's about the actions you take. Consistency is what bridges the gap between what you promise and what you deliver. It's about showing up, day in and day out, with the same commitment to your values, your team, and your mission. When you lead by example consistently, you set the standard for everyone else. People trust leaders who walk their talk, and that trust becomes the foundation for a strong, motivated, and aligned team.

### Why Consistency Matters

Imagine a leader who preaches the importance of punctuality but frequently shows up late to meetings. Or someone who talks about teamwork but never collaborates or shares credit. Those mixed signals create confusion, resentment, and a lack of respect. People are watching you as a leader, even when you don't realize it. Your actions speak louder than your words, and inconsistency erodes trust faster than anything else.

Consistency gives people something solid to rely on. When your team knows what to expect from you, they feel more secure and confident in their own roles. It's not about being perfect, it's about being steady. For example, if you value transparency, consistently share updates with your team, even when the news is difficult. If you emphasize work-life balance, show your team that you respect those boundaries by not sending emails at midnight or working through weekends.

Consistency also builds credibility. Over time, people start to believe in you not just because of what you say, but because of what you've shown them through your actions. It's this credibility that earns you the benefit of the doubt when challenges arise or when you need your team to rally behind a tough decision.

## The Practical Side of Leading by Example

Leading by example isn't just about the big, dramatic gestures, it's about the small, everyday actions that add up over time. For instance, if you expect your team to prioritize customer service, make sure you're personally modeling that behavior. Respond to customer concerns promptly and with empathy, even if it's not "your job." When your team sees you going the extra mile, they'll be inspired to do the same.

Consistency also means showing up with the same energy and focus, even when you're having a bad day. Everyone has off days, but as a leader, you set the emotional tone for your team. If you're constantly moody or unpredictable, your team will feel like they're walking on eggshells. On the other hand, if you approach each day with steadiness and composure, you create a sense of stability that keeps the team grounded.

It's important to note that consistency doesn't mean rigidity. Situations change, and good leaders adapt. The key is to be consistent in your principles, even if your tactics need to evolve.

For example, if your company is going through a major shift, you might need to adjust priorities or change processes. But if you've consistently been transparent and communicative in the past, your team will trust you to guide them through the transition with integrity.

## Building a Culture of Consistency

When you lead by example, you're not just shaping your own behavior, you're setting the tone for the entire team. Consistency becomes contagious. When people see that you follow through on your commitments, they're more likely to do the same.

Take accountability as an example. If you make a mistake, own up to it. Say, "I dropped the ball on this, and here's how I'm going to fix it." That honesty and accountability show your team that it's okay to acknowledge mistakes and focus on solutions. Over time, this creates a culture where people feel safe to take responsibility, rather than hiding errors or pointing fingers.

Consistency also means being fair and equitable in how you treat your team. If you hold one person accountable for missing a deadline, but let someone else slide for the same behavior, you send the message that favoritism is at play. Treating everyone with the same level of respect and expectation reinforces the idea that everyone is part of the same mission.

Another way to lead by example is by maintaining your own growth and development. If you expect your team to learn new skills or adapt to changes, show them that you're doing the same. For instance, if your organization is implementing a new tool or system, don't just delegate the training, attend it yourself. Show your team that you're willing to put in the work alongside them.

## The Long-Term Impact of Consistency

Leading with consistency doesn't just make you a better leader, it transforms your team. Over time, your actions create a culture of trust, accountability, and excellence. Your team knows they can count on you, and that reliability becomes a model for how they approach their own work.

The long-term impact is especially powerful during times of change or crisis. When people are uncertain about the future, they look to their leaders for stability. If you've built a reputation for being consistent, your team will feel reassured, even when things are tough. They'll know that, no matter what happens, you'll lead with integrity and stay true to your values.

Ultimately, consistency is about legacy. It's about the example you set today that shapes the leaders of tomorrow. Your actions, repeated over time, become the stories your team tells about you, the lessons they carry forward and the standards they hold themselves to. Leadership isn't about occasional heroics, it's about showing up every day with the same commitment, the same values, and the same drive to make your team better. That's the power of consistency, and that's how you build something that lasts.

4

# Empowering Your Team to Take Ownership

One of the most powerful moves you can make as a leader is to empower your team to take ownership of their work. Leadership isn't about controlling every little detail or being the hero of every project. It's about unleashing the potential within each individual, giving them the confidence and freedom to make decisions, learn from mistakes, and grow. When you empower your team, you create an environment of accountability, collaboration, and trust. People don't just work for you: they work with you, and that's where the magic happens.

## Leading by Empowering, Not Micro-Managing

If you want to get the best out of your team, stop controlling every aspect of their work. Micromanaging is one of the fastest ways to crush morale, stifle creativity, and destroy productivity. It's not just frustrating for the people on your team, it's draining for you as well. The constant need to oversee every detail means you're spending your time stuck in the weeds, rather than leading with purpose and focus. And let's be real, it's exhausting! So, how do you shift from micromanaging to empowering? It's all about giving your people the autonomy to make decisions, trusting them to take ownership of their roles, and leading with the mindset that everyone on your team is capable of contributing in meaningful ways.

## The Myth of Control

One of the biggest mistakes leaders make is thinking that if they aren't constantly overseeing every project, things will fall apart. This is the lie we tell ourselves to justify micromanaging. We think that by having control over every aspect of the work, we ensure perfection. The truth is, the more you try to control, the less control you actually have. You limit the creativity, initiative, and problem-solving abilities of your team by not giving them the freedom to think for themselves.

Think of it like this: when you micromanage, you are treating your team as if they're incapable of doing their jobs without your constant oversight. You've essentially created a work environment where people don't feel trusted to make decisions, and that's a productivity killer. Instead of fostering responsibility, you're breeding dependence.

Let's look at a real-world example: if you're working with a marketing team and you give them a clear brief, but then hover over every design or copywriting decision, they won't feel empowered to do their best work. They'll second-guess their decisions because they're waiting for your approval at every step. If instead, you empower them by giving them ownership over the project, providing them with the resources they need, and trusting their abilities, they'll be more creative, confident, and committed to delivering great results. When you take a step back and stop micromanaging, you give your team the space to shine.

## Trusting Your Team to Lead

Empowering your team starts with trust. If you don't trust them to do their work, then you'll never be able to step back and lead effectively. But trust isn't a "one-time" thing, it's built over time through consistent actions and behaviors. When you trust your team, you stop being the bottleneck in every decision. You allow your team to make choices, solve problems, and face challenges without your constant intervention.

For example, imagine you're working with someone on a complex project. Instead of jumping in and taking control when things get difficult, you offer support in the form of guidance and feedback. You step in when necessary but trust your team to make decisions. You empower them by reinforcing that they are capable of handling the challenges that come their way. You're providing them with the opportunity to learn and grow in real time, rather than waiting for you to swoop in and fix everything.

Building trust with your team isn't just about believing in their skills, it's about showing them that you believe in their potential to solve problems, make decisions, and innovate. When you remove the constraints of micromanagement, you unleash your team's creativity and allow them to take ownership of the work.

## The Power of Accountability

Empowerment doesn't mean abandoning accountability, it means sharing ownership. When you empower your team, you still hold them accountable for results but you do so in a way that encourages growth, rather than stifling it with unnecessary oversight. The key is to set clear expectations and then give your team the autonomy to meet them.

A great example of this is when you give someone ownership of a project but still expect them to report on progress. This is where the fine line between empowerment and micromanagement lies. You can set clear milestones or deadlines, but instead of hovering over their every move, you let them work toward those goals independently. If something goes off track, you provide feedback, but you don't micromanage every step of the process. You're still holding them accountable, but you're also empowering them to find their own solutions along the way.

The more you show that you trust your team to handle their responsibilities, the more likely they are to step up. Empowerment breeds a sense of ownership and pride. When people know they are accountable for their work, they feel a deep sense of responsibility, which leads to better performance and higher levels of engagement.

## Shifting From Control to Coaching

The best leaders don't focus on controlling the work, they focus on coaching their teams to success. Instead of hovering over every task, you guide and mentor your team. You provide them with the knowledge, skills, and resources they need to succeed. You ask questions that help them think critically, rather than giving them all the answers. This shift from controlling to coaching is essential for creating a culture of empowerment.

A coaching mindset encourages your team to think for themselves. Instead of telling them how to solve every problem, you ask questions like, "What do you think the best approach is?" or "How do you plan to tackle this challenge?" This empowers them to take ownership of the solution, rather than relying on you to make decisions for them. It's a shift that builds both confidence and competence within your team.

This approach also means creating a feedback loop. You don't just check in on your team's progress, you provide constructive, actionable feedback to help them improve. You celebrate their successes, but you also help them navigate failures without shame. You view mistakes as learning opportunities, not as evidence of incompetence. That's how you build a high-performing team: by giving people the tools to succeed and the confidence to lead.

**The Long-Term Impact of Empowerment**

When you start empowering your team, it doesn't just benefit the individuals, it transforms the entire organization. You'll see people rise to challenges, take ownership of their roles, and innovate in ways they never would have if you were always hovering. You'll create a culture of trust, accountability, and collaboration. And most importantly, you'll start seeing results that go beyond just meeting deadlines! You'll create a team that's fully engaged, motivated, and committed to the success of the organization.

Empowerment also has a massive impact on retention. When people feel trusted and valued, they're more likely to stay loyal to the company. They'll be less likely to burn out because they feel supported and recognized for their contributions. You're not just getting the best out of your team in the short term, you're building long-term loyalty and commitment.

In the end, when you lead by empowering, not micromanaging, you create an environment where everyone thrives. Your team takes ownership, they grow, and they start driving results with a level of passion and commitment that can't be matched when you're constantly pulling the strings. As a leader, your job is not to control every action. Your job it's to guide, support, and trust your team to make the best decisions. The power of empowerment is limitless, and when you embrace it, you unlock the true potential of your team.

## Developing Leaders Within Your Team

As a leader, one of your primary roles is to develop other leaders. If you're the only one leading in the organization, you're limiting growth, both for your team and for yourself. A true leader doesn't just build their own influence, they build a culture of leadership that permeates throughout the entire team. When you focus on developing leadership within your team, you're not just grooming people for future positions, you're building a high-performing, self-sustaining team that can handle challenges, take ownership, and drive results without relying on constant direction from you. This is how you create a lasting impact, not just as a manager, but as a leader who builds legacies.

**Identifying Leadership Potential**

Not everyone is born a leader, but everyone has the potential to be one. The first step in developing leaders is identifying who has leadership potential within your team. Leadership potential isn't just about who's the most vocal, the most confident, or the person who's been in the industry the longest. It's about spotting qualities that go beyond technical skills. Leadership potential shows up in small, everyday behaviors: taking initiative without being asked, being willing to help others without expecting anything in return, staying calm in high-pressure situations, and having the ability to inspire others to take action. These qualities aren't necessarily flashy, but they are foundational for future leaders.

Look for the team members who are already influencing their peers, those who quietly make things happen without needing to be told. They are often the ones who step up during tough times, who show responsibility even when it's not required, and who rally others around a common goal. These people may not necessarily be the loudest or most outspoken, but their actions speak volumes.

Start by engaging these individuals in regular conversations about their aspirations. Understand what excites them about their work and where they see themselves growing in the future. You'll begin to identify who has the drive and potential to step into a leadership role. And remember, leadership is not just about title, it's about the ability to inspire, influence, and guide others toward success.

## Providing Opportunities for Growth

Once you've identified potential leaders, the next step is providing them with the right opportunities for growth. Leadership development isn't a one-size-fits-all approach, but it does require intentional action. Look for ways to provide exposure to different aspects of the business. If you want someone to become a great leader, you can't just have them sit in the same role forever. You need to challenge them, expose them to different projects, and stretch their capabilities.

Consider giving potential leaders ownership of a project or task that involves cross-functional collaboration. This will expose them to different parts of the business, help them develop new skills, and teach them how to influence others without relying on authority. If you have a team member who's showing potential, let them lead a small group on a particular project or ask them to take charge of a new initiative. This doesn't mean throwing them into the deep end with no support, it means offering guidance and mentorship while giving them the space to grow and learn from the experience.

This might also include encouraging them to take on new challenges that push them outside their comfort zones. For example, if one of your team members has shown potential but lacks experience in managing people, give them the opportunity to manage a small team or lead a meeting. It's these real-world experiences that accelerate leadership growth. While it's easy to stick with what's comfortable, it's through challenging moments that future leaders really start to step up.

As you provide opportunities, make sure to offer continuous

feedback. Leadership is a journey, and it's important to give people regular input on their strengths and areas for improvement. The feedback should be constructive, supportive, and designed to help them understand where they can grow. Encourage them to keep challenging themselves and reassure them that failure is part of the learning process.

**Coaching and Mentorship: Developing Leadership Skills**
Developing leaders within your team is not just about giving them more responsibilities, it's about coaching them, guiding them, and providing mentorship. True leadership development requires ongoing support. It's not about handing someone the reins and expecting them to know everything, it's about teaching them the skills, mindset, and strategies they need to thrive.

Start by creating a mentoring relationship with emerging leaders. This is where you can really make an impact. Rather than just delegating tasks or giving assignments, sit down with your team members and help them understand the deeper principles of leadership. Share your experiences, mistakes, and lessons learned. Talk to them about the mindset required to lead: how to make tough decisions, deal with conflict, or communicate effectively with others. Share stories of how you've navigated difficult situations, and make it clear that leadership isn't about being perfect, but about showing up consistently and authentically.

Leadership coaching should be an ongoing process. Regular check-ins are essential to help your potential leaders refine their skills. In these meetings, you can discuss their challenges, goals, and progress. Give them guidance on how to manage people, inspire teams, and drive results. It's about offering the support they need, when they need it, and helping them build the confidence to lead on their own.

An important part of mentorship is also helping your team members develop emotional intelligence, the ability to manage their emotions and understand others' emotions. A great leader is empathetic, self-aware, and emotionally resilient. These qualities are just as important as technical skills, if not more. To help your emerging leaders develop emotional intelligence, encourage them to be reflective, practice active listening, and take ownership of their emotional responses. By coaching them on these soft skills, you're helping them build a strong foundation for effective leadership.

## Creating a Leadership Culture

Once you start developing leaders within your team, it's time to create a culture where leadership is a shared responsibility, not just something for a few select individuals. Leadership should be seen as a set of behaviors and skills, not a title. When you foster this culture, everyone on your team becomes a potential leader.

A culture of leadership encourages open communication, shared responsibility, and mutual support. It's about creating an environment where everyone feels empowered to lead, even if they don't have formal authority. Encourage collaboration and make it clear that everyone's input is valuable. Create opportunities for everyone to take the lead on projects, share ideas, and make decisions.

Leadership also means taking ownership. By embedding ownership at every level, you show your team that they are responsible for the outcomes they create. When leaders at all levels take ownership, you create a sense of accountability that drives success throughout the organization.

Celebrating leadership at all levels is crucial. Recognize people who show leadership behaviors, even if they're not in managerial roles. Praise those who step up in challenging moments, who help others without being asked, and who consistently drive results. By recognizing these behaviors, you reinforce the idea that leadership isn't confined to a few, it's something that can be developed and demonstrated by anyone on the team.

## The Long-Term Impact of Developing Leaders

When you develop leaders within your team, you're setting the stage for long-term success not just for the individuals, but for the entire organization. Empowering people to lead creates a ripple effect that can transform the culture of your company, making it stronger, more resilient, and more adaptable to change.

As these leaders grow and take on more responsibility, they become your trusted partners, and you free yourself up to focus on strategic goals, business development, and larger initiatives. You don't have to be the only one leading. You've created a leadership ecosystem, a web of individuals who are all working toward the same vision, taking ownership of their roles, and pushing the organization to new heights.

Developing leaders within your team also ensures the sustainability of your organization. When everyone in your organization is a potential leader, you create a culture of continuous improvement and innovation. Your team doesn't just follow orders, they're empowered to lead change, drive progress, and contribute to the organization's success on a deeper level.

The process of developing leadership within your team is one of the most rewarding investments you can make, both for your organization and for your own growth as a leader. It's about creating a legacy that extends beyond your tenure and impacts the future of your team and the broader company.

## Fostering a Collaborative, High-Performance Environment

If you want your team to achieve at the highest level, you need to foster a collaborative, high-performance environment. But here's the thing: collaboration doesn't just mean getting together for meetings or brainstorming sessions. **True collaboration happens when people from different backgrounds, with different skill sets and perspectives, come together to create something greater than the sum of its parts**. When you create an environment where collaboration thrives, it becomes a space where ideas flow freely, trust is built, and teams are aligned on a common vision.

A high-performance environment doesn't happen overnight, and it doesn't rely on just getting the best talent in the door. It's about creating a culture where people are empowered to perform at their highest level, where they trust each other, hold each other accountable, and support one another through every challenge. So, how do you do this? How do you build a team that consistently outperforms the competition, supports each other, and thrives under pressure? It starts with the right leadership, the right systems, and a deep commitment to creating a culture where everyone is pulling in the same direction.

**Building Trust Through Open Communication**
**Collaboration starts with trust, and trust starts with open, transparent communication**. If your team doesn't feel like they can speak freely, they won't share ideas, they won't ask for help when they need it, and they won't take risks. This is why it's so critical to create an environment where communication is encouraged, not just in meetings but in everyday interactions.

As a leader, you have to set the tone for open communication. It's on you to model honesty and transparency. Share what's happening within the organization, keep your team informed about both successes and challenges, and be candid about your expectations. The more transparent you are, the more your team will feel like they're trusted, and the more they'll be willing to collaborate.

It's also important to create opportunities for your team to communicate openly with each other. Facilitate conversations between departments or across different levels of the team. Collaboration happens when people are given the space and the platform to connect, exchange ideas, and work toward common goals. Break down silos within your team by encouraging cross-functional collaboration, even if it's something as simple as organizing team-wide updates or brainstorming sessions. The more you get people talking, the more opportunities for collaboration you create.

One powerful way to foster communication is through feedback. Encouraging a feedback-rich environment where feedback is both given and received regularly can help people feel more comfortable sharing ideas, voicing concerns, and stepping outside their comfort zones. But this doesn't mean just waiting for formal performance reviews. Feedback should be an ongoing, two-way street that happens constantly. By creating a safe space for both positive and constructive feedback, you encourage a culture where people are open to learning and improving together.

## Aligning on Common Goals and Vision

Collaboration can't happen unless everyone is on the same page. For people to work together effectively, they need to understand the bigger picture: the common goal they're working toward. Without alignment, individual efforts will be scattered, and the team will be pulling in different directions. This is where leadership comes in: it's your job to ensure that your team is aligned with the vision and that everyone knows how their work contributes to that vision.

Start by clearly articulating the goals of the team and the organization. Make sure these goals are not only shared but understood by everyone, from the newest team member to the most senior leader. If the vision is fuzzy or the goals are unclear, your team will struggle to collaborate effectively. It's about providing clarity and purpose so that everyone knows what success looks like and how they fit into that picture.

When your team is aligned on common goals, collaboration becomes much easier. People stop seeing each other as competitors and start seeing each other as teammates working toward the same end result. Everyone starts pulling in the same direction, and that collective focus leads to greater results. This alignment also helps when challenges arise. If your team knows what they're working toward, it's easier to rally together, problem-solve, and find creative solutions to obstacles.

This alignment can be reinforced through regular check-ins and updates. Keep your team focused on the big picture by consistently reminding them of the larger goals and vision. It's not just about saying, "Here's what we're working on." It's about constantly linking back to the why. "Here's why we're doing this, and here's how it contributes to the overall success of the company." This clarity creates a sense of ownership, accountability, and motivation that drives high performance.

## Encouraging Diverse Perspectives and Creativity

One of the most powerful ways to foster collaboration is by encouraging diverse perspectives. When everyone on your team thinks the same way, innovation stalls. Diverse perspectives come from people with different experiences, backgrounds, and ways of thinking, and they're essential for creative problem-solving. A team that thrives in a high-performance environment needs a mix of people who approach challenges differently, think outside the box, and bring unique ideas to the table.

To build this kind of diversity, start by hiring with intention. Bring people on board who can contribute different viewpoints and experiences. Don't just hire people who look like you, think like you, or have the same background. Look for candidates who will challenge the status quo, who will bring something new to the table.

But it's not just about diversity of background, it's about creating a culture where diverse ideas are welcome. People need to feel comfortable sharing their thoughts, even if they're not fully formed or "perfect." Encourage brainstorming sessions where every idea, no matter how unconventional, is valued. This gives people the freedom to think creatively without fear of judgment.

As a leader, you can encourage this creativity by asking thought-provoking questions. Rather than just telling your team what to do, ask them, "What's the best way we could tackle this?" or "What ideas can we explore to improve this process?" These questions open the door for innovative thinking. They encourage your team to come up with ideas themselves and bring their creativity into the conversation. When people feel like their input matters and is valued, they'll be more likely to contribute and collaborate.

## Recognizing and Celebrating Team Contributions

Collaboration isn't just about working together, it's about recognizing and celebrating the contributions that each team member makes toward collective success. When people feel like their efforts are acknowledged, they're more motivated to continue working hard, collaborating, and striving for excellence.

As a leader, make it a point to celebrate wins, big or small, both as a team and individually. Publicly acknowledge team members who go above and beyond, who collaborate seamlessly, and who contribute great ideas. The more you celebrate collaboration, the more your team will buy into the idea that success is a team effort, not an individual pursuit.

But recognition isn't just about pats on the back. It's about rewarding teamwork in a way that reinforces collaboration. This could be through team bonuses, recognition programs, or simply taking time to say thank you. Celebrating success together strengthens the bond between team members, builds a sense of shared achievement, and makes people feel appreciated.

When people feel appreciated and recognized, they become more motivated to perform at their highest level. They see that their contributions are meaningful and that they are part of something bigger than just their own work. This sense of purpose fuels high performance, and it strengthens the collaborative spirit that drives the entire team toward success.

**The Impact of a Collaborative, High-Performance Culture**
A culture of collaboration and high performance doesn't just benefit individual team members, it benefits the entire organization. When teams are aligned, communication is open, creativity is encouraged, and contributions are celebrated, the result is a team that can achieve extraordinary things.

By fostering collaboration, you create a workplace where

people are motivated to do their best work, where they feel like their ideas matter, and where they trust each other to succeed. It's an environment where everyone is pulling in the same direction, with a shared sense of purpose and commitment to excellence. This kind of culture doesn't just lead to improved performance, it leads to innovation, growth, and sustained success.

As a leader, when you focus on collaboration and high performance, you're building a team that doesn't just work together, you're building a team that thrives together, that supports each other, and that creates exceptional results. And that's the key to building a long-lasting, high-impact organization.

## Recognizing and Celebrating Team Achievements

One of the most powerful ways to keep a team motivated, engaged, and high-performing is by consistently recognizing and celebrating their achievements. But here's the truth: recognition isn't just about handing out praise after big milestones. It's about building a culture where every contribution is seen, valued, and celebrated. People want to feel like their work matters. They want to know that the effort they're putting in is being noticed and that it contributes to something bigger than just themselves. Recognition isn't just a nice-to-have, it's essential for creating an environment where people are encouraged to keep pushing boundaries and striving for excellence.

But, here's the kicker: **it's not just about the "big wins." It's about acknowledging the small wins, too**. Every step forward, every challenge overcome, and every collaborative effort should be celebrated. When you as a leader focus on celebrating these moments, you instill a sense of pride and ownership in your team, and that drives continued success. People will work harder when they know their efforts are being seen, appreciated, and celebrated.

## Acknowledging Individual and Collective Efforts

Recognition starts by understanding that the team's success is built on both individual and collective contributions. Each person brings their unique skills, perspective, and effort to the table, and each one deserves recognition. Celebrating both individual and team achievements creates a balanced environment where people feel personally valued while also understanding the importance of teamwork.

For individuals, take the time to acknowledge specific contributions. If someone went above and beyond to help the team meet a deadline, share that acknowledgment with the whole group. Not only does it show the person who contributed that you notice their efforts, but it also highlights the behaviors you want to see repeated. Be specific about what they did well, whether it was their creativity in solving a problem, their persistence in overcoming challenges, or their willingness to support teammates.

However, celebrating individual contributions doesn't mean leaving the team out of the equation. A high-performing team is one that works together to achieve common goals. Celebrate the collective efforts that made a big win possible, and make sure that every person who contributed to that success feels recognized. When you celebrate the team's achievement, you reinforce that the group is greater than the sum of its parts. This collective recognition creates a sense of unity and reinforces the idea that everyone's role is integral to the success of the whole.

A simple "Thank you" in a team meeting, a shout-out in an email, or even a handwritten note can go a long way. Recognition doesn't always need to be elaborate. It's the thought behind it that counts, the message that says, "I see you, and what you did matters."

## Public Recognition: Elevating Team Morale

Public recognition can be one of the most effective ways to boost team morale. When people are celebrated in front of their peers, it not only makes them feel appreciated but also sets an example for the rest of the team. Public recognition signals that excellence is noticed and valued. It motivates others to strive for similar recognition, and it builds a culture of excellence where everyone feels driven to contribute their best.

As a leader, you have many ways to publicly recognize achievements. You can do this in team meetings, on internal communication channels, in company newsletters, or through team-wide emails. If you have a company-wide platform or intranet, use it to highlight accomplishments across teams. Share success stories, whether they're big or small, and make sure to give credit where it's due.

Be sure to focus on how individual actions or collective efforts have impacted the team or company as a whole. Celebrate the "why" behind the achievement. Did someone's contribution help speed up a project or reduce costs? Did they find a creative solution to a problem that was holding the team back? When people understand how their actions affect the broader organization, they feel a deeper sense of purpose and pride in their work.

For example, if a team meets a project deadline early, don't just thank them for their hard work, talk about the impact that early completion has on the company's broader goals. If one team member helped another team solve a problem, celebrate how this collaboration has contributed to the overall success of a larger initiative.

The key is to make recognition public and specific, so everyone knows what's being celebrated and why it's important. Public recognition builds trust and transparency and creates a ripple effect of positive behavior.

**Celebrating Milestones and Achievements Big and Small**

Recognition should be an ongoing process, not just something that happens when there's a major milestone or big project. Acknowledging everyday achievements can have just as much of an impact on the team's morale as celebrating big successes. Consistent recognition reinforces positive behavior, strengthens relationships, and fosters a culture of mutual support.

Celebrating even the smallest of wins can make a huge difference. Maybe someone hit a personal best on a target or overcame a significant challenge. Maybe a team member went the extra mile to help a colleague. These are moments worth celebrating. Acknowledge these wins, whether it's through a quick email, a note of appreciation, or a quick mention in a team meeting.

Celebrating key milestones, too big wins, like project completions, revenue targets being hit, or a new product launch, should be recognized publicly. But it's also about marking progress along the way. Celebrate the journey as much as the destination. When people see that the small victories matter, it keeps them motivated and pushes them to keep performing at their best.

For example, if your team completes the first phase of a big project, take the time to recognize that milestone. Yes, the final project outcome is important, but the progress along the way matters too. It's the momentum you build in these smaller, incremental victories that will carry you to the final goal.

Celebrating milestones doesn't always have to be done in formal settings. It could be as simple as a celebratory lunch, an afternoon off, or even a casual team gathering. The idea is to create a positive atmosphere that reinforces the idea that success is worth celebrating. Recognizing the hard work that gets you to the finish line is as important as celebrating the final win.

## Meaningful Rewards and Incentives

While recognition is important, rewards can also play a crucial role in reinforcing the behaviors you want to see in your team. Rewards don't always have to be monetary or extravagant, but they should be meaningful. A good reward system helps reinforce the idea that success has tangible benefits, and it shows the team that their hard work is appreciated in ways that go beyond just words.

Start by understanding what motivates your team. Some people thrive on public recognition, while others prefer more private acknowledgment. Some may be motivated by tangible rewards, like gift cards or extra time off, while others may find a reward like a development opportunity, mentorship, or an expanded role more meaningful. Get to know your team's preferences, and tailor rewards to individual needs.

Incentives can also take the form of professional development opportunities. A high-performing employee might appreciate the chance to attend a conference, take a leadership course, or work on a special project. For others, a reward might be the chance to take on a challenging new responsibility that aligns with their career goals.

Celebrating achievement with meaningful rewards motivates the team to keep pushing toward success. It shows that hard work doesn't just go unnoticed, it's something that's actively valued and appreciated.

## Creating a Culture of Continuous Recognition

Building a culture of recognition isn't just about moments of celebration, it's about making recognition part of the fabric of your organization. When recognition is ingrained into your company's culture, it becomes automatic. People start recognizing and appreciating each other without needing to be prompted, and the behavior becomes self-sustaining.

You can build this culture by leading by example. As the leader, be the first to recognize others. Acknowledge their efforts, contributions, and successes as they happen, both publicly and privately. Encourage your team to do the same. When recognition becomes a part of daily interactions, it reinforces the idea that success, no matter how big or small, should be celebrated and appreciated.

Additionally, create systems that make recognition part of the organizational workflow. Whether it's an internal recognition platform where team members can give kudos to one another, or a monthly team meeting where individual and team successes are celebrated, find ways to integrate recognition into your team's routine.

A culture of continuous recognition breeds positivity, loyalty, and a commitment to high performance. When your team knows that their efforts will be celebrated, they are motivated to keep putting in the work. They'll feel empowered to keep striving for excellence, knowing that their contributions will always be noticed and valued.

# 5

# Sustaining Long-Term Success and Growth

As a leader, you're not just in it for the short-term wins. Sure, the immediate results are gratifying, but what really sets you apart is how you maintain momentum and sustain long-term success. It's not just about making the numbers look good now, it's about creating a system that empowers your team, fosters growth, and builds a legacy of leadership that lasts far beyond the immediate challenge. Sustaining success takes more than just hard work, it's about creating an environment where people can thrive, innovate, and grow. Consistently!

The beauty of leading with kindness and assertiveness is that, when done right, it doesn't just drive immediate success, it lays the foundation for sustainable growth. Leading with empathy, transparency, and clear boundaries doesn't just motivate people in the moment, it builds trust, loyalty, and a culture where growth is the natural next step.

# Building Long-Term Relationships with Your Team

Building long-term relationships with your team is not just about having friendly conversations or being there for them when things get tough. It's about creating deep, meaningful connections that foster trust, loyalty, and a sense of shared purpose. These relationships are the bedrock of a high-performing, engaged team. If you want to sustain success over the long haul, you need to focus on building a foundation where team members feel valued, respected, and heard. And that doesn't happen overnight.

Real, lasting relationships take time, effort, and a commitment to understanding each individual on your team not just as employees but as people. When you take the time to build these relationships, you create an environment where people feel emotionally invested in the work, in the team, and in your shared goals. And the return on investment is huge. People who feel like they have a genuine relationship with their leader are more likely to stay engaged, work harder, and go above and beyond.

## Understanding Your Team Beyond the Workplace

Building meaningful relationships starts by seeing your team as more than just a group of workers. They are human beings with their own dreams, challenges, aspirations, and personal lives. A leader who takes the time to understand these aspects is able to connect on a deeper level and create a work environment where people feel genuinely valued.

The first step in building these relationships is to get to know your team members outside of their job descriptions. Find out what they're passionate about, what excites them, and what drives them. Ask about their goals not just professionally, but personal. What are their long-term career aspirations? What do they want to achieve in their lives? What hobbies or interests do they pursue outside of work?

By getting to know these details, you show your team that you care about them as people, not just employees. This understanding creates a sense of trust, and trust is the key to any successful relationship. When people trust you, they are more open, more willing to collaborate, and more motivated to contribute to the team's success.

## Consistent Communication and Active Listening

One of the most important aspects of building long-term relationships is maintaining consistent communication. But communication isn't just about speaking, it's about listening, too. If you're constantly talking but not actively listening to your team, you're missing a huge opportunity to build stronger relationships.

Make it a priority to regularly check in with each team member, not just in formal settings like one-on-ones or meetings, but in casual conversations, too. The best leaders are those who make themselves approachable and available for their teams, whether it's for work-related concerns or just to talk about life. These informal interactions help build trust and rapport and give your team a sense of connection to you beyond just the job.

In these conversations, practice active listening. This means really focusing on what the person is saying without interrupting or thinking about what you're going to say next. Acknowledge their feelings and provide thoughtful responses. Ask follow-up questions to show that you genuinely care about their perspective. When your team members feel heard, they will feel respected and valued. This creates an open, honest dialogue that strengthens relationships and fosters a culture of trust.

## Showing Up When It Matters

Building long-term relationships with your team requires you to be there for them, not just when things are going well, but especially when they're going through tough times. Real relationships are tested in moments of crisis, challenge, or uncertainty. It's easy to be a great leader when everything is running smoothly, but true leadership is shown when things get difficult.

Be present for your team during tough moments, whether it's helping them navigate a personal crisis, offering guidance during a work-related challenge, or providing support when they're feeling overwhelmed. Your presence in these moments shows your team that they matter to you beyond their productivity or results. This is where the real bonds are formed.

For example, if one of your team members is struggling to balance work and personal life, take the time to check in and offer support. Maybe they need flexibility in their schedule, or maybe they just need someone to listen. By offering a helping hand, you show that you care about their well-being. When your team sees that you're there for them in the good times and the bad, it builds loyalty and deepens the relationship.

## Leading with Vulnerability

A huge part of building long-term relationships is leading with vulnerability. Vulnerability in leadership doesn't mean weakness, it means being human, showing your team that you're not perfect, and being open about your own struggles and challenges. This openness fosters a sense of authenticity and encourages your team to be open with you in return.

By showing vulnerability, you set the tone for a culture where people feel comfortable being themselves. When they see that you're willing to be real and transparent, they feel safer doing the same. It removes the walls between you and your team, making you more relatable and building trust.

For example, if you've made a mistake, don't be afraid to own up to it. Acknowledge it, learn from it, and use it as a teachable moment. Share what you've learned from your failures, and encourage your team to do the same. This vulnerability doesn't make you less of a leader, it makes you more effective, because it creates a sense of camaraderie. Your team knows you're in it with them, not above them.

## Providing Growth and Development Opportunities

One of the best ways to build long-term relationships with your team is by investing in their growth. Show your team that you care about their future by providing opportunities for professional development, mentorship, and skill-building. When you invest in someone's growth, it signals that you see potential in them and are committed to helping them reach their goals.

This doesn't just mean offering formal training programs or workshops. It means taking the time to guide, mentor, and challenge your team members in their day-to-day roles. Help them take on new responsibilities, expose them to new challenges, and provide feedback that helps them grow. When people feel like their growth matters to you, they're more likely to invest their time and energy into helping the team succeed.

Mentorship plays a huge role in this. Find ways to mentor your team members whether that's through regular check-ins, providing constructive feedback, or offering guidance on their career trajectory. When people see that you care about their development, they feel a sense of loyalty to you and the team. This loyalty will carry over to the long-term success of your group.

## Consistency and Reliability

Finally, building long-term relationships means being consistent and reliable. Your team needs to know that they can depend on you. If you say you're going to do something, do it. If you promise to provide feedback, do it. If you commit to supporting your team through challenges, follow through.

Reliability is a huge trust-builder. If you're inconsistent, your team will feel uncertain, and that uncertainty can erode the foundation of your relationships. On the other hand, when you show up consistently and honor your commitments, your team knows they can rely on you. This reliability builds trust and strengthens the relationships you have with your team over time.

## Continuous Improvement Through Feedback and Reflection

As a leader, one of the most powerful tools you have in your arsenal is the ability to foster continuous improvement not just in your team, but in yourself as well. The world around us is always changing. The marketplace, customer expectations, and team dynamics are in a constant state of flux. In order to thrive in this environment, it's not enough to rely on past successes or lean on outdated strategies. You need to actively seek ways to improve, adapt, and grow. This is where feedback and reflection come in.

The beauty of continuous improvement is that it is an ongoing cycle, never-ending, always evolving. By embracing feedback and reflection, you not only create an environment where your team can grow but also model the behavior you want to see in them. The result is a culture of growth, innovation, and relentless pursuit of excellence.

Feedback isn't just about what's wrong, it's about growth. It's about sharpening skills, identifying opportunities, and building better systems. And reflection isn't about self-criticism, it's about taking the time to pause, think deeply, and learn from every situation, every success, and every failure. Together, feedback and reflection form the foundation for a culture where continuous improvement is not just encouraged but expected.

## Embracing a Feedback-Rich Culture

If you're not actively seeking feedback, you're missing out on the most direct and effective way to grow. But feedback, in order to be meaningful, needs to come from the right place and be delivered the right way. As a leader, your job is to create a culture where feedback is not feared or avoided but actively sought after and embraced.

The first step in creating this feedback-rich culture is to model it yourself. Leaders who are open to feedback demonstrate vulnerability and a commitment to growth. If you expect your team to be receptive to feedback, you need to show that you're also willing to accept it. This means asking for feedback on your leadership style, your decision-making, and how you're supporting the team. Don't wait for annual reviews! Feedback should be constant, real-time, and integrated into daily work life.

Take the initiative to ask questions like: "How can I support you better?" or "What do you think about how I handled that situation?" This openness not only sets the tone for your team but also allows you to stay in tune with how they're feeling and where improvements can be made. When feedback is part of the regular conversation, it becomes less of a confrontation and more of a natural, constructive part of the team dynamic.

Encourage your team to provide feedback to one another, too. Create an environment where feedback is seen as an opportunity for growth, not criticism. When team members provide feedback to each other in a supportive, solution-oriented way, it leads to improved communication, better teamwork, and stronger relationships. You want to build a space where team members feel comfortable pointing out issues, suggesting improvements, and learning from each other.

Ultimately, feedback should be seen as a gift, a tool for continuous improvement. It's about identifying what's working well and what's not, and taking actionable steps to get better. And this mindset needs to be embedded in your team culture if you want to see sustainable, long-term growth.

## The Power of Regular Reflection

While feedback is essential for identifying areas of improvement, reflection allows you to process that feedback, make sense of your experiences, and come to better conclusions. Reflection is a tool that allows you to step back from the day-to-day grind and analyze what worked, what didn't, and why. It helps you see the bigger picture and make adjustments that will lead to more effective leadership in the future.

Reflection isn't just about reviewing the facts, it's about connecting the dots. Take time to think deeply about your actions and decisions. Ask yourself questions like: "What could I have done differently in that situation?" "How did my team respond to my leadership today, and why?" or "What can I do to improve my approach tomorrow?" These reflective moments give you the insight needed to adjust and recalibrate your strategy.

But reflection doesn't just apply to you as a leader, it applies to your entire team. Encourage your team members to reflect on their work, their projects, and their own performance. This can be done through regular retrospectives or one-on-one meetings where the focus is on learning and growth. Ask your team to reflect on what went well, what challenges they faced, and how they can improve in the future. This not only helps individuals develop their skills but also allows the entire team to learn and grow together.

Reflection also provides clarity when it comes to long-term goals. It helps you and your team track progress over time and adjust course when necessary. When you regularly reflect, you can spot patterns, identify what's working, and eliminate what's not. It's a way to course-correct without waiting for a major crisis to unfold.

**Leveraging Feedback and Reflection for Personal Growth**

As a leader, you can't expect your team to improve if you're not actively working on your own growth. Continuous improvement starts with you. By actively seeking feedback and making time for reflection, you can constantly evolve your leadership style, improve your decision-making, and refine your approach to managing your team.

After all, leadership is not a static role, it's dynamic. The needs of your team will change over time, the business landscape will shift, and the challenges you face will evolve. In order to navigate these changes, you need to be adaptable, and that requires personal growth. Seeking feedback is one way to ensure that you're aware of where your weaknesses lie, so you can address them head-on. Reflection gives you the time and space to process that feedback and make the necessary adjustments.

For example, if you've received feedback that you're not as clear in your communication as you could be, take time to reflect on specific instances when this happened. Why was that the case? How can you ensure that your communication improves moving forward? Is it a matter of clarity in your messaging, or is it about listening more actively to your team's needs? Reflection allows you to analyze situations in greater detail and come up with solutions that will benefit both you and your team.

Ultimately, continuous improvement is a process that takes time and requires dedication. It's a commitment to growth, both for yourself and for your team. By regularly seeking feedback, reflecting on your experiences, and being open to change, you create an environment where growth is not just a goal, it's a culture.

## Making Feedback and Reflection a Habit

To truly reap the benefits of feedback and reflection, you need to make them habits, not just one-off exercises. The more feedback you ask for, and the more regularly you reflect on your experiences, the more natural these practices will become.

Start by incorporating feedback and reflection into your daily routine. Set aside a few minutes each day to reflect on your actions and decisions. At the end of each day, ask yourself what went well and what could have been better. Take note of patterns that emerge and make adjustments as needed. Similarly, make it a habit to regularly check in with your team, asking for their feedback and providing them with constructive insights.

You can also establish regular feedback sessions within your team. Hold brief, informal check-ins where everyone has a chance to give and receive feedback. You don't need to wait for a formal meeting or performance review to discuss how things are going. The more feedback you give and receive, the more it becomes a natural part of the team culture.

Incorporating feedback and reflection into your daily life not only drives improvement but also helps you build stronger relationships with your team. They'll appreciate your openness and commitment to their growth, and you'll lead by example. Over time, these habits will help you become a more effective leader, and they'll set your team up for success.

## Overcoming Challenges in Leading with Kindness

Leading with kindness is one of the most powerful leadership approaches you can adopt, but that doesn't mean it's without its challenges. The idea of being kind as a leader may sound like a no-brainer, but in practice, it's not always as simple as it seems. You might find yourself questioning whether you're being "too nice," or whether your kindness is being taken advantage of. You may struggle with balancing kindness with the need to hold your team accountable. These are real concerns, but they are also part of the growth process of becoming the kind of leader who inspires and motivates others.

Being a kind leader doesn't mean letting go of authority, nor does it mean avoiding difficult conversations. In fact, kindness is often tested in the toughest moments. It's easy to be kind when things are running smoothly, but true leadership shines when you face challenges when your kindness is stretched, and you have to make tough decisions while still maintaining your humanity.

The good news is that you don't have to sacrifice kindness to be effective. Kindness can coexist with strong leadership, accountability, and decisiveness. The key is understanding how to navigate these challenges and stay true to your values. So, let's dive into the most common obstacles you may face when leading with kindness, and how to overcome them.

**Balancing Kindness with Accountability**

One of the biggest challenges you'll face as a kind leader is balancing kindness with the need to hold people accountable. You might worry that being too empathetic or understanding could lead to lax performance standards, or that showing compassion might come across as weakness. This is a common misconception that many leaders face when they try to lead with kindness.

The truth is, kindness doesn't mean avoiding accountability. In fact, some of the most effective leaders are those who hold their teams accountable while maintaining a supportive, empathetic environment. The key here is understanding that accountability isn't about being harsh or punitive, it's about helping your team understand expectations, providing them with the support they need to meet those expectations, and holding them to a high standard in a constructive, respectful way.

When someone on your team is underperforming, the kindest thing you can do is address the issue head-on. But instead of criticizing or reprimanding, approach the situation with empathy and a solution-oriented mindset. Have a one-on-one conversation where you ask questions like, "What challenges are you facing?" or "How can I support you to improve in this area?" By focusing on the person and their needs, rather than just the issue, you maintain a compassionate, yet accountable, leadership style.

**Remember, accountability doesn't have to be aggressive.** It's about being clear with expectations, providing feedback, and offering the tools your team needs to succeed. When people feel safe and supported, they are more likely to take ownership of their performance and improve.

**Overcoming the Fear of Being Perceived as "Too Nice"**
Another challenge you may face as a kind leader is the fear of being perceived as "too nice" or too lenient. There's a stereotype that kindness in leadership is a sign of weakness, or that it leads to a lack of control. You may worry that if you show too much empathy or warmth, your authority will be undermined. This is a real concern, but it's based on the misconception that being kind means being passive or permissive.

In fact, the most successful leaders are often those who lead with both kindness and confidence. Leading with kindness doesn't mean you let people walk all over you. It means that you approach people with respect, build relationships, and create a supportive environment where individuals feel valued and empowered. Kindness and strength can coexist, one reinforces the other.

You can be kind and still set clear boundaries and make tough decisions when necessary. When you lead with kindness, you don't need to yell, belittle, or intimidate to get results. Your authority comes from your clarity, your values, and the respect you've built over time.

To overcome the fear of being perceived as "too nice," remind yourself that kindness is a powerful tool, not a weakness. When you're genuinely invested in your team's success and well-being, they'll respect you more for it, not less. By modeling kindness, you encourage a positive, respectful work culture where people want to perform at their best. You'll attract loyalty and dedication, which are far more valuable than the fear-based compliance that comes from an authoritarian style of leadership.

**Navigating Tough Conversations with Empathy**
As a kind leader, you'll inevitably encounter situations where difficult conversations are required whether it's giving tough feedback, addressing a team member's behavior, or having to let someone go. These conversations are some of the hardest you'll face as a leader, and they can test your commitment to kindness.

In these moments, you might feel conflicted. You want to show compassion, but at the same time, you need to maintain a level of professionalism and ensure that you're addressing the issue at hand. So how do you navigate tough conversations while remaining kind and empathetic?

The key is to approach these conversations with honesty,

respect, and a solution-oriented mindset. Even when the conversation is uncomfortable or confrontational, kindness doesn't mean avoiding the issue, it means addressing it with care.

For example, when giving tough feedback, focus on being clear and constructive. Instead of simply pointing out what went wrong, frame the conversation around how things can improve. Provide specific examples and suggest actionable steps for growth. Always balance critique with appreciation. For instance, "I noticed you missed a few key deadlines, but I also know you've been working hard on the project. Let's talk about what we can do to improve the situation moving forward."

Empathy in these situations doesn't mean sugar-coating the truth, but rather acknowledging the other person's feelings and perspective. By showing that you care about the person's experience and their growth, you keep the relationship intact, even while addressing tough issues.

When it comes to firing someone or making other difficult decisions, kindness doesn't mean avoiding the hard conversation, it means having it with humanity and respect. Give the person the dignity they deserve, and offer support for their transition if possible. If you approach these situations with kindness, you maintain trust, and your team will see that you make tough decisions in the best interest of the team and the individual.

**Managing Your Own Emotional Reactions**
Leading with kindness also means managing your own

emotional reactions. As a leader, you're constantly navigating high-pressure situations, and sometimes your emotions can get the best of you. When you're under stress, it's easy to react impulsively or get frustrated with your team. But in those moments, your emotional state can impact how your team views your leadership and how they respond to you.

To lead with kindness, you need to be self-aware and regulate your emotions. This doesn't mean suppressing your feelings, it means responding to situations thoughtfully, even when you're under pressure. Take a breath before reacting, and ask yourself how you want to handle the situation. When you're calm and composed, you set the tone for the rest of your team.

Being able to manage your emotions allows you to show up with consistency, even in difficult situations. It also allows you to model emotional intelligence for your team. When they see you handling stress or conflict with grace, they'll be more likely to adopt similar strategies for managing their own emotions.

## The Long-Term Benefits of Leading with Kindness and Assertiveness

Leading with both kindness and assertiveness isn't just a leadership style, it's a powerful, long-term strategy that pays off in ways that go beyond short-term results. When you embrace this dual approach, you create a ripple effect that impacts everything from team morale to performance, to the culture of your entire organization. It's an investment in the sustainability of your leadership, the growth of your team, and the success of the organization as a whole.

Kindness and assertiveness may seem like opposites at first glance, but when combined, they form a balanced and highly effective leadership approach. Kindness fosters a culture of trust and openness, while assertiveness ensures clarity and accountability. Together, they create a thriving environment where individuals feel valued, motivated, and empowered to contribute their best work. So, let's take a deeper look at the long-term benefits of leading with kindness and assertiveness.

## Stronger, More Loyal Teams

One of the most significant long-term benefits of leading with kindness and assertiveness is the loyalty you build within your team. People want to work for leaders who treat them with respect, listen to their concerns, and support their personal and professional growth. When you lead with kindness, you show your team members that they are more than just employees, they're valued individuals with unique skills and potential.

Kindness helps you build strong, personal relationships with your team, which fosters trust. When trust is present, people feel comfortable being open with you, sharing their ideas, and even offering constructive feedback. They understand that their contributions are appreciated, and this recognition leads to deeper loyalty.

But loyalty isn't just about being nice. Assertiveness plays a crucial role here too. By being clear about expectations, holding people accountable, and making decisions that are in the best interest of the team and the organization, you demonstrate that your leadership is rooted in fairness and integrity. When you lead with both kindness and assertiveness, your team knows where they stand. They respect your authority because it's balanced with empathy. They know you care, and they trust you to make decisions that are both supportive and fair.

The result is a team that sticks together, that trusts each other, and that works towards common goals with a shared sense of purpose. Loyal teams are not only more engaged but also more productive. They're motivated by a leader who balances kindness with clear direction and accountability, creating a stable and supportive work environment where people want to contribute their best.

## Improved Communication and Collaboration

When kindness and assertiveness are at the core of your leadership, communication improves dramatically across the board. Kindness encourages openness and transparency, while assertiveness ensures that communication is direct, clear, and actionable.

When you communicate with kindness, you foster an environment where people feel heard and valued. This means they're more likely to speak up when they have ideas, share concerns when something's not working, and collaborate with their peers to solve problems. You create an atmosphere of psychological safety, where people feel free to express themselves without fear of judgment or retribution.

At the same time, assertiveness ensures that communication is effective and efficient. You don't just want people to speak up, you want them to speak with clarity and purpose. Being assertive means that you're able to communicate your ideas and expectations in a way that others can understand and act upon. This creates alignment, reduces misunderstandings, and helps everyone stay on the same page.

When kindness and assertiveness work together, the result is a team that communicates openly and honestly. Collaboration becomes easier because people trust each other's intentions, and they understand exactly what's expected of them. Clear communication leads to faster decision-making, smoother workflows, and stronger partnerships both within your team and across the organization.

## A Culture of Innovation and Growth

Leaders who combine kindness and assertiveness create an environment where innovation thrives. Kindness encourages creativity by allowing people to feel supported in sharing their ideas. When your team knows they won't be shut down or dismissed for offering a new idea, they are more likely to think outside the box, take risks, and try new approaches to solving problems.

But innovation doesn't happen without accountability. Assertiveness ensures that ideas are executed with precision, and that the focus remains on achieving results. Assertive leadership means you can push your team to move beyond just generating ideas to actually implementing them. It's about taking action and driving progress, which keeps the momentum for innovation alive.

When these two qualities are combined, you create a culture that values both creativity and results. Employees feel empowered to contribute their best ideas, knowing that they will be taken seriously, while also understanding that there are clear expectations for following through. This kind of culture leads to continuous improvement, higher levels of performance, and greater success over time. It's a culture where people feel supported, challenged, and encouraged to reach their full potential.

**Long-Term Employee Satisfaction and Retention**

When you lead with kindness and assertiveness, you're investing in the long-term well-being of your employees. **Kindness helps create a work environment where employees feel seen, heard, and respected, which directly contributes to their overall job satisfaction**. People are more likely to stay at a company where they feel valued and where they have a leader who genuinely cares about their growth and development.

Assertiveness, on the other hand, provides structure and clarity. Employees appreciate knowing where they stand, what's expected of them, and how their contributions align with the organization's goals. When your leadership is clear and consistent, it minimizes uncertainty and helps employees feel more secure in their roles. They know they're working towards a shared vision, and they understand how their individual efforts contribute to the team's success.

This combination of kindness and assertiveness leads to higher employee satisfaction and retention. People are more likely to stay at a job where they feel they are treated with respect and have the opportunity to grow. This is crucial in today's job market, where employees often seek more than just a paycheck, they want to feel like they're part of something meaningful.

## Sustainable Results and Business Growth

While kindness and assertiveness certainly lead to improved team dynamics and individual satisfaction, they also have a profound impact on the long-term success of the business. When you build a culture of trust, clear communication, innovation, and accountability, you create a foundation for sustained business growth.

A team that feels supported, motivated, and aligned with the company's mission is far more likely to deliver consistent results. Leaders who lead with kindness and assertiveness make decisions that balance short-term objectives with long-term sustainability. They know that building a thriving organization isn't about quick wins, it's about creating a strong, enduring foundation that will carry the business forward for years to come.

The long-term benefits of leading with kindness and assertiveness include not just higher profits but also a reputation for being a company that invests in its people. In an era where companies are judged not just by their bottom line but also by their corporate values and how they treat their employees, leading with kindness sets you apart. It's not just the right thing to do, it's a strategic advantage.

6

# Leading with Kindness and Assertiveness The Journey Ahead

**F**irst off, **I want to thank you**. *Thank you* for sticking with me through this journey. We've explored the power of leading with kindness and assertiveness, and now it's time to take that knowledge into the real world. But before we wrap up, let's take a moment to recap where we've been and acknowledge what lies ahead.

Kind and assertive leadership is not just an ideal, it's the blueprint for creating high-performing, thriving teams. We've seen that when you lead with both compassion and clarity, you build trust, foster accountability, and empower your team to take ownership of their roles. We've discussed how kindness doesn't mean being weak and how assertiveness doesn't mean being harsh. The two can, and should, go hand in hand to create an environment where people not only respect you as a leader but are also inspired to do their best work.

But here's the thing: ***It's not always going to be easy***. No matter how much we believe in the power of kind and assertive leadership, there will be days when you don't feel like yourself. Some days, you'll be exhausted, frustrated, or overwhelmed. And some days, the people you work with will challenge your patience and test your leadership style. It's normal, and it's human.

What matters most is **how you show up on those days.** Remember, you don't have the same predisposition every single day, and neither do the people you're leading. The key to successful leadership is not perfection, it's consistency and adaptability. It's about recognizing the tough days and using them as opportunities for growth, both for yourself and your team.

I encourage you to take everything you've learned in this book and put it into practice. Have conversations about these principles with the people you work with. Discuss how you can implement more kindness and assertiveness into your day-to-day interactions. It's through those discussions that real change happens! When you start to challenge old habits and reinforce new, healthier leadership dynamics.

And if you've found value in this book, I'd be so grateful if you could leave a review on Amazon. Your feedback helps others in the leadership community find the tools they need to be the leaders they were meant to be. Reviews also give this book the opportunity to reach more people who are ready to break away from outdated, ineffective leadership practices and embrace a new way forward: one that combines strength with compassion.

Thank you once again for reading, for engaging, and for taking the time to grow as a leader. I believe in you, and I know that with this approach, **you're not just going to lead your team, you're going to transform it.**

Now, go lead with purpose, lead with kindness, and lead with unwavering assertiveness. The future of leadership is yours.

## References

*Be a kind leader rather than a nice leader | Lead Read Today.* (2022, December 14). Lead Read Today | Fisher College of Business. https://fisher.osu.edu/blogs/leadreadtoday/be-a-kind-leader-rather-a-nice-leader

Bissinger, B. (2024, June 17). *Leading with Kindness: Transforming Your Leadership Style.* Align. https://aligntoday.com/blog/leading-with-kindness

Gadeyne, S. (2023, April 21). *Kindness in Leadership: Why Prioritizing kindness Can benefit your business.* https://www.linkedin.com/pulse/kindness-leadership-why-prioritizing-can-benefit-your-seija-gadeyne/

Hr, H. (2024, September 3). *A kind leader is not a "Soft" leader: How kindness delivers phenomenal value for people and business.* https://www.linkedin.com/pulse/kind-leader-soft-how-kindness-delivers-phenomenal-value-people-t3yoe/

Trotta, J. (2024, August 8). Why kindness matters for effective leadership - Emergenetics. *Emergenetics.* https://emergenetics.

com/blog/why-kindness-matters-for-effective-leadership/

75